Anke Weiland

The Treaty of Waitangi

GRIN Verlag

Bibliografische Information der Deutschen Nationalbibliothek:

Die Deutsche Bibliothek verzeichnet diese Publikation in der Deutschen National-
bibliografie; detaillierte bibliografische Daten sind im Internet über http://dnb.d-
nb.de/ abrufbar.

Imprint:

Copyright © 2010 GRIN Verlag GmbH
Druck und Bindung: Books on Demand GmbH, Norderstedt Germany
ISBN: 978-3-656-74198-5

This book at GRIN:

http://www.grin.com/en/e-book/280063/the-treaty-of-waitangi

GRIN - Your knowledge has value

Der GRIN Verlag publiziert seit 1998 wissenschaftliche Arbeiten von Studenten, Hochschullehrern und anderen Akademikern als eBook und gedrucktes Buch. Die Verlagswebsite www.grin.com ist die ideale Plattform zur Veröffentlichung von Hausarbeiten, Abschlussarbeiten, wissenschaftlichen Aufsätzen, Dissertationen und Fachbüchern.

Visit us on the internet:

http://www.grin.com/

http://www.facebook.com/grincom

http://www.twitter.com/grin_com

Maori wellbeing, including concerns such as education, health, reasonable incomes or appropriate participation in political discussions were important matters when the Treaty was drafted. Maori had been able to manage all those issues on their own and their methods were quite advanced. Having a look at the Maori fisheries for example, Cook claimed when he arrived in 1769 that 'he was highly impressed by the sophistication of Maori fishing compared to their own primitive gear' (Hersoug 2002). Besides that, also the social organisation of the business was well developed (Hersoug 2002). Things changed as soon as foreigners, namely the British arrived in New Zealand and 'discovered' this country. With this arrival, things in New Zealand became different. Due to the fact that there were no laws to which the british settlers felt bounded, they acted the way they wanted. Besides that, the French and the Americans started to peer at this land beeing lately added to the world map. At this time, the Crown felt constrained to take actively action on the situation. The document which turned out oas a result of this situation was the Treaty of Waitangi. Drawing observance to the Aborigine Act, the Treaty would recognize certain rights of the natives, including the issues mentioned at the very beginning. Besides that, the Treaty 'guaranteed full rights of ownership of their lands, forests, fisheries and other prized possessions' (Orange 2004) to Maori people. As the fisheries are a part of the guaranteed rights mentioned in the Treaty, they may be taken to examine the current impact of the Treaty in New Zealand society.

Observing the impacts of the present times the Treaty has on Maori fisheries chronologically, it seems logical to start with the Quota Management System (QMS) which had been introduced in 1986 (Durie 2006). Having a look at the Treaty principle of Article two which claims 'full exclusive and undisturbed posession of lands and estates, forests, fisheries, and other properties' (Durie 2006), the QMS breaches the Treaty. Yet before the British arrived in New Zealand, there was already a Fish Trading bussines between the tribes, which proves that the 'Maori fishing interests were commercial in nature' (Durie 1998). When conceptualizing the QMS, the traditional Maori fishing interests were categorized as "customary". Therefore, in the understanding of the people who drafted the QMS, the Treaty would grant the Natives the right to retain fishing for subsistence. Hence, the breach of the Treaty is therefore due to the presumption that Maori fisheries had only been substantial, which is not correct. In the light of that there can be found several evidence for the opposite.

Besides that, the provison of Article three, assuring "royal protection" occurs to be inadequat with the QMS. In relevance to this provision, it would have been the duty of the Crown to make sure that Maori rights were not affected by any Acts. Actually, the Crown showed no responsibility in terms of Maori fisheries nor tried to prove the situation of Maori fisheries was different from what the QMS imputed to the natives.

Due to the just mentioned disagreements, the Muriwhenua claim came up just in the year of the introducement of the QMS, arguing that it appears inappropriate with the rights the Treaty guaranted Maori people. As the QMS would not consider the Maori having had fisheries in terms of trade and in addition the Crown or the government was just selling rights and licences and therefore corportarising fishing, the Muriwhenua claim requested that Maori fisheries had to stand outside the QMS (Durie 1998). Bringing up that claim to the Waitangi Tribunal, the findings argued, amongst other things with the traditional views and beliefs of the Natives, that neither the land belonged to anyone, and therefore nor do the forests or the fisheries (Waitangi Tribunal 1998). This finding appears rather invalid in terms of arguing that corportarising the fisheries was a legal act. If fisheries belong to no one, then the selling of that property which belongs to no one appears impossible. In conclusion, arguing with the criteria of the Treaty or the traditional views of Maori, the QMS seems to threaten the Treaty principles and violates Maori rights.

Quite the same discrepancies can be found in terms of the Fisheries Act from 1983. In the face of that, this Act 'presumed Maori interests to be of a subsistence nature and therefore limited' (Durie 2006). It ignores the evidence of pre-existing, sophisticated and well organised fishing businesses, evident from before the signing of the Treaty, as well as does the QMS. Having again a look at the principle of Article two in the Treaty that guarantes "full and undusturbed posession", the dissonance with the Treaty is proved. Furthermore, the Fisheries Act itself turns out to be dissonant in itself by endorsing 'Nothing in this Act shall affect any Maori fishing rights' (Durie 2006).

Maori were unwilling to disclaim the rights which were given to them when they signed the Treaty of Waitangi. To give them anything less would be in direct conflict with the Treaty. Concerning Article two that claims "full and undisturbed posession", the Maori disapproved the QMS as they felt their rights were curtailed. Based on the provision of the Treaty, Maori claimed at least and not less than 50 percent of the Quota, what seems already to be a compromise. In accordance with the Treaty that both parties signed, the Maori rights were supposed to be "full" and "undisturbed", not "half", nor "shared". Therefore, claiming only a share of their rights, the Maori had already legally conceded a part of the fisheries to the government, part of the land and the rights that belonged, according to the Treaty, to them.

However, what the Natives got out of that claim is the Fisheries Act from the year 1989. This document awards the new Maori Fisheries Comission about 10 per cent of the Quota and besides that, supplies about ten million NZ Dollar to Aotearoa Fishing, a company owned by the comission (Durie 1998). Paying attention to the fact that Maori claims were, besides that they were well founded, already just claims for a compromise, the quota of ten per cent and a nonrecurring payment turns up as a unjustified admittance. Relating the Fisheries Act of 1989, to the Treaty of Waitangi it seems complicated to locate Treaty provisions or principles in that document.

As another important cornerstone in this discussion about the relevance of the Treaty in concerns to Maori fisheries, may the year 1992 be recognized. Still unsatisfied with the QMS and the Fisheries Act and therefore the rights or better regulations and restrictions those documents gave to Maori, the Sealords Deal was drafted. Agreeing at the point that overfishing caused serious problems and therefore the envirnoment and the fishstocks are badly affected by that, the aim that both parties had in common was to strive for a sustainable use of the sea and the fisheries. There was much less consensus between the two parties as to who should cut down the fisheries. Drawing attention to the provision of article two of the Treaty, the government conded several, but not all of the rights the Treaty admitted Maori. To finally bring the discussion to an end, the government wanted Maori to agree, after granting them 20 per cent of the QMS and providing 150 million NZ dollar, that no more claims would be brought up about fisheries in the courts and Waitangi Tribunal. By using the money the government provided, Maori would be able to 'enter into a joint venture purchase of Sealords Ltd.' (Durie 1998), a company which was holding 26 per cent of the quota. Besides that, the Natives were also awarded to 20 per cent of every new species of fish that would occur. This deal seemed not to be the ideal solution, but several iwi considered it as the best solution that could be achieved, even if it was costly to the Treaty rights (Durie 1998). In comparison to the situation as it used to be before the Sealords Deal, an improvement is beyond doubt perceivable. Compared to the ten per cent of the quote Maori used to have, they gained another 26 per cent from the joint venture with Sealords Ldt., and in addition they could record another ten per cent gain in the quota, what adds up, together with the 1.5 per cent Moana Pacific was holding, to a total of 37.5 per cent. In conclusion this means that Maori became, by confirming the Sealords Deal, the biggest alottee of the Quota (Durie 2006). However, concerning the acceptance of the Sealords Deal that it was supposed to achieve amongst the tribes, the success appears rather failed. Taking a look at the figures and therefore

4

beeing only able to record that '16 out of 54 tribes approved the agreement' (Durie 1998: 158) does not give an impression of a succsesfuly accomplished mission. In fact, as the validation of the Sealords Deal may have actually been beholded, nevertheless we may not forget that not all Maori signed the Treaty, and that not even a third of those who signed the Treaty were positivley tempered in terms of the Sealords Deal. Relating this fact to article three of the Treaty, which guarantees Maori the same rights as British citizens and therefore the right to democratie, it appears questionable if this third article has not also come to know a breach.

In conclusion, it is evident that Maori have been subject to many changing policies regarding their fisheries and have experienced injustice in terms of what is rightfully entitled to them. Maori view themselves as guardians of the land, including fisheries, and to see the depletion of fishing resources under Crown authorities gretly pained them. By way of the terms of the Treaty of Waitangi Maori are entitled to the "full exclusive and undisturbed possession" of their taonga, including their fisheries. In fact, what Maori got out of several Fisheries Acts or the Sealords Deal is not equivalent to what the Treaty guaranted them. The results of those Acts and Deals recognizes the Treaty in a way, but does not fulfill the allowance the Treaty entitles Maori. Besides that, the Crown failed to protect the rights of the Natives by not interfering and, even more grave, did not support Maori when they brought up their claims to the Waitangi Tribunal. Even if the Crown did not actively act against Maori claims, it may be considered as a failure not to act at all. Inequitable besides that appears the fact that the land, or better the sea and the fishstocks which were destroyed actually belonged or should legally belong to the Maori, the Natives of New Zealand.

References

Durie M. 1998. Te Mana, Te Kawanatanga. The Politics of Maori Self-Determination. Oxford University Press. Melbourne.

Durie, M. 2006. Nga Tai Matatu. Tides of Maori Endurance. Oxford University Press. Singapore.

Hersoug, B. 2002. Unfinished Business. New Zealand's experience with rights-based fisheries management. Eburon Delft. Delft.

Orange, C. 2004. The Treaty of Waitangi. Bridget Williams Books Limited. Wellington.

Waitangi Tribunal. 1988. Muriwhenua Fishing Report. Government Printing Office. Wellington.